simply r

{HEARTSPA™}

Relational Bible Series for Women

MW01037114

Group

Loveland, Colorado

simply relevant
{HEARTSPA™}
Relational Bible Series for Women

Credits

Author: The Lovely Linda Bever
Editor: Amber "Snaps" Van Schooneveld
Senior Editor: Amy "Danger" Nappa
Copy Editor: Jovial Julia Wallace
Chief Creative Officer: Joyful Joani Schultz
Art Director and Cover Art Director and Designer: Artsy Andrea Filer
Production Manager: DeAnne Lear

ISBN 978-0-7644-3444-0
10 9 8 7 6 5 4 3 2   16 15 14 13 12 11 10 09
Printed in the United States of America.

Contents

Welcome to Simply Relevant: HeartSpa™! This is your totally relevant six-week Bible series that will help you develop relationships with other women as you grow in your relationship with God. OK, so what's a Bible series got to do with a spa, you ask? Well, this series is all about how we find refreshment in Jesus—how much he wants to renew and bless us. And what better metaphor for that than a spa?

A spa-themed Bible series also gives women who aren't quite convinced about coming to a church activity that extra little nudge to come. Paul's words, "I try to find common ground with everyone, doing everything I can to save some" (1 Corinthians 9:22) have never been so nicely applied!

Each week you'll learn about a different aspect of God's refreshment and how it applies to your life. You'll explore how to find rest in Jesus; you'll reflect on where you've turned for rest in the past; and you'll learn about God's healing, how we are refreshed in relationships, and how we can bring the message of Christ's living water to others. Whew! That's a long list, so we've given you pampering spa activities to deepen and enrich your learning in a way you can really understand.

You can do this Bible series with five to 50 women—or even more! And you want women to really grow in relationships with each other, so remember to get in small groups of four or five for discussion if you have a larger group. Women at any place in their faith journeys can feel right at home with this Bible series. The discussion questions can be understood and applied by women who don't know Jesus yet or women who are long-time friends with him. All the Bible passages are printed out for you, so those who aren't familiar with the Bible have the verses right in front of them.

So what will you be doing each week? Here's the structure of the sessions:

Note to the Hostess

Your hostess will be the woman facilitating your Bible series. She'll read the session through before the meeting, prepare for the activities, gather any supplies needed, and get the snacks ready. This box contains special tips just for the hostess, such as supplies to gather for the Experience, the atmosphere for the week, and ideas for snacks.

Mingling

Each week, you're going to start with snacks, mingling, and a short prayer. And this is key: Take time to share how you did with your previous week's commitment.

Experience

Together, each week you'll engage in an experience that will bring a new depth of meaning to the topic you'll explore. The experiences will get every woman involved and having fun. There might be a little bit of preparation or supplies needed, which the hostess will supply.

The Word

Each week, you'll read a Scripture passage together and then discuss what it means with questions from this guide. The questions are surprising, personal, and relevant to women today.

A Closer Look

This is a quick look at the Bible passages you'll be digging into each week. You can read this box together during the session or on your own at home. These insights will help you develop a deeper understanding of the verses at hand while discussing their meaning in your lives.

Take Action

This is where women put faith into action. You'll all commit to apply what you've learned in the coming week in a practical way. You can write your own commitment or choose from the suggested commitments. Then next week, you'll check in with each other to see how you did.

Prayer

At the end of each session, you'll spend time in prayer together. You can ask for prayer requests and also pray about the commitments you've made for the upcoming week. We've also given you a verse to read together to focus your minds for prayer.

Girlfriend Time

If you want some more hangout time together after your session is over, we've given you fun suggestions for easy activities to do together to reinforce the session's topic or to just relax. This is an optional bonus that will help you grow deeper in your friendships.

Still Thirsty?

If you want to explore the week's topic more, we've given you additional verses and reflection questions to read and consider in the coming week.

We pray that in the next six weeks, this study will help you grow as friends of Jesus and each other, and, most of all, learn to be refreshed in Jesus daily!

—Group's Women's Ministry Team

Rest

Finding Rest in Jesus

Note to the Hostess:

OK, it's time to pamper the socks off your friends. Since this is the first meeting, go the extra mile to create an atmosphere that will relax women and prepare them to rest in God. They may be coming from screaming babies, demanding bosses, or road ragers.

Create a haven of tranquility with low lighting, a few flickering candles, and soft music. If you have a small desk fountain, place it in your meeting area. (It'll really emphasize the theme.) And serve simple spa snacks to set the mood, such as bottled water or herbal tea, cucumber rounds topped with store-bought red pepper hummus, and fresh fruit.

Get It...Got It?...Good.

- refreshing spa snacks
- flickering candles
- stopwatch or clock for the Experience section
- cucumber slices for Girlfriend Time (optional)

Mingling

Enjoy the snacks and make sure you all know each other's names. Need a little help? Here's a conversation starter:

Hi, my name's [your name], and when I really need to rest, I:

Before starting, pray something like this:

> *God, thank you for bringing each individual woman here. Help us to put everything that's crowding our minds aside so that we can find our rest in you. In Jesus' name, amen.*

Experience

(Note: The hostess will prepare this experience.) Many of us have *heard* over and over about how God gives us rest—so much so that our eyes glaze over when we hear those words before really giving a second thought to what they mean. Do this activity that will help you *experience* what it feels like to have your burdens lifted.

Get into groups of three and stand next to one another. Have the two women on the outside hold down the middle woman's arms while she tries as hard as she can to raise them to the side. Use a clock or stopwatch, and have women let go of their partners' arms after 30 seconds. Switch roles so that each woman gets to be in the middle.

Ahh, didn't it feel good to have your burdens lifted?

Q: Quick, name all of the words that come to mind that describe how it felt to have your arms held down.

Q: How about when your arms were released?

Q: When have you felt like this after having a burden in your life lifted?

the Word

Read Matthew 11:28-30 together:

Matthew 11:28-30

Then Jesus said, "Come to me, all of you who are weary and carry heavy burdens, and I will give you rest. Take my yoke upon you. Let me teach you, because I am humble and gentle at heart, and you will find rest for your souls. For my yoke is easy to bear, and the burden I give you is light."

a closer look

Matthew 11:28-30

Read this box anytime to take a deeper look at the verses for this session.

Today's passage focuses on finding rest in Jesus by taking on his "yoke." Which may lead you to wonder…what's a yoke?

A yoke is a wooden harness or frame that fits over the neck and shoulders of animals to make them work together. The yoke is attached to a plow or other farming tool that is pulled by the animals. Most of the time the Bible uses this imagery to refer to slavery or difficult times. Yet in this passage, Jesus says his yoke is a *positive* thing.

Many of us are yoked to heavy burdens. Life feels difficult. We have burdens of sin. People are demanding and it weighs us down. We're weary of searching for answers. Jesus, with *his* yoke, frees us from these heavy burdens and gives us his rest through our relationship with him. Let's find out how as we open God's Word together!

scripture discussion questions

In groups of four or five, discuss these questions:

Q: What kind of burdens do you think Christ is talking about in this passage?

Q: What burdens are you carrying that are really wearing you out?

Q: How do the words you thought of in the experience of having your arms held down relate to this?

Q: Jesus said, "Let me teach you, because I am humble and gentle at heart, and you will find rest for your souls." What other teachings, teachers, or methods of teaching might he be comparing himself to?

Q: Notice that Jesus doesn't *just* say that he will give us rest. His words indicate that we gain his rest by taking on his yoke. What does it mean to take on Jesus' yoke?

heartfelt tip

The word *yoke* in the Old and New Testament didn't just refer to a physical burden—it also was a symbol of oppression and the heavy burden of the legalistic teachings of some rabbis (1 Kings 12:4, Acts 15:10). Jesus compares the heavy burdens of legalism—having to do a bunch of stuff to be good enough—to coming to follow him and his teaching: They are "easy" and "light" and will give you rest.

Q: Compare receiving Jesus' rest with the experience of having your arms released.

Q: Are you ready to stop carrying your burdens on your own and take on Jesus' yoke? If not, what's stopping you? If so, how can you do this?

Take Action

Let's not just *talk* about finding rest for our souls in Jesus, *let's do it!* Write below how you're going to trade your weariness and burdens for Jesus' yoke and rest. If you're having a hard time thinking of something, choose one of the ideas below. Next week, you'll share with one another how you did.

this week

○ I'm going to give my burdens to Jesus and take on his yoke and rest by:

....

....

....

....

○ I'm going to sit down and write out an honest list of all my reasons for not setting down my burdens and accepting Jesus' gift of rest. Then I commit to have a long honest talk with God about them.

○ I commit to let Jesus teach me in his humble and gentle way. I'll read Matthew 6:25-34 to learn more about resting in God and meditate on what that means for my life.

○ I'll gather a few pebbles to carry in my pocket. Each time I find myself picking up my burdens, I commit to stop in my tracks. I'll take out a pebble and pray that God will help me put the burden back down and instead take on Jesus' yoke and his rest. Then I'll throw that pebble away.

Prayer

End your time together in prayer to your Father.
Read Psalm 139:1 together.

> O Lord, you have examined my heart and know everything about me.

God knows every little thing about us—every burden, every worry, every fear. Approach him with the confidence of much loved daughters. He's calling out to you to rest in him! Thank him that he'll take your burdens and give you rest, and commit to find your rest in him alone, taking on Jesus' yoke.

Girlfriend Time

When your time of study is over, relax together with this pampering activity. Place slices of cooled cucumbers over your eyes, lean back on some pillows, and rest. While your eyes are closed, take turns telling the person reclining next to you about what's happening in your life. Then listen to her share. Enjoy this time of calm and rest together before heading back to the "real" world.

Still Thirsty?

If you're still thirsty to know more about the rest God offers you, check out these Scriptures:

Exodus 20:9-11

"You have six days each week for your ordinary work, but the seventh day is a Sabbath day of rest dedicated to the Lord your God...For in six days the Lord made the Heavens, the earth, the sea, and everything in them; but on the seventh day he rested. That is why the Lord blessed the Sabbath day and set it apart as holy."

Q: The Lord doesn't need rest, right? But he rested on the seventh day. Why do you think?

Psalm 68:19

"Praise the Lord; praise God our savior! For each day he carries us in his arms."

Q: Imagine being carried in someone's arms. How do you feel? How is this like what you should feel every day as God carries you?

Jeremiah 6:16

"This is what the Lord says: 'Stop at the crossroads and look around. Ask for the old, godly way, and walk in it. Travel its path, and you will find rest for your souls. But you reply, "No, that's not the road we want!" ' "

Q: Sometimes walking our own path *seems* so much easier than following God's path. Do you find true rest when going your own way?

Philippians 4:6-7

"Don't worry about anything; instead, pray about everything. Tell God what you need, and thank him for all he has done. Then you will experience God's peace, which exceeds anything we can understand. His peace will guard your hearts and minds as you live in Christ Jesus."

Q: This verse says God's peace is an experience. How do you not just *know* about God's peace but really *experience* it?

1 Peter 5:7

"Give all your worries and cares to God, for he cares about you."

Q: Why give your cares to God? Why not someone else? Who might you be tempted to give your cares to instead of God?

Reflect

Note to the Hostess:

This week is a time for introspection, so create an atmosphere in which women can be relaxed and reflective. Use indirect lighting, such as candles. Trickling water from a desk fountain and soft, slow-paced instrumental music can create the right mood for reflection.

Serve cold lemon-mint water (lemon slices and fresh mint leaves provide a refreshing taste and color contrast) and a colorful dessert such as sponge cake with whipped cream, topped with sliced berries and a sprinkle of powdered sugar. Make it look and taste mouthwatering!

Get It...Got It?...Good.

- mood setters from last week and indirect lighting
- soft, instrumental background music
- mouthwatering dessert; lemon slices and fresh mint leaves
- stopwatch for the Experience section

Mingling

Before you enjoy the snacks the hostess has prepared, pray something like:

Thank you, God, for bringing each of us back together today. Our lives have been so busy. Please help us to relax so we can listen to your words for us. In Jesus' name, amen.

Now indulge in the refreshing dessert and beverage. If you're still learning one another's names, introduce yourselves by saying:

Hi, my name's [your name]. When I'm really hungry, my all-time favorite meal is:

Then share with each other how you did with last week's Take Action commitments, how you gave your burdens to Jesus and found his rest.

Experience

(Note: The hostess will prepare this experience.) Noise and confusion surrounds us these days. Silence rarely happens in our fast-paced culture and our everyday lives. Sometimes we feel tension mounting inside us and don't even know why. Let's experience an activity that will help us understand what God means when he asks us to reflect and listen to him.

Take about a minute to name noises you heard today (crying baby, loud music, construction work).

Then, as the Hostess keeps time, sit in total silence for 60 seconds.

Now find a partner and face each other. Take a moment to think of a significant event in your life. For the next 60 seconds, on cue, everyone look into the eyes of your partner and tell your experience *out loud, simultaneously.*

Whew! Take a breath. Now recap your important event to each other, *one partner at a time,* this time listening to understand one another. (Take about two minutes each.)

Then, with your partner, discuss these questions:

Q: How did you feel in you sat in silence? Was the silence productive? Did time pass quickly or did it drag on?

Q: What words pop into your head that describe how you felt when everyone was talking at once?

Q: As your partner retold her story, what did you have to do to really listen and understand her? How is this similar to listening to God?

the Word

Read Isaiah 55:1-2 together:

Isaiah 55:1-2

Is anyone thirsty? Come and drink—even if you have no money! Come, take your choice of wine or milk—it's all free! Why spend your money on food that does not give you strength? Why pay for food that does you no good? Listen to me, and you will eat what is good. You will enjoy the finest food.

a closer look

Read this how anytime to take a deeper look at the verses for this session.

Today's passage is God's personal invitation to you to forget that stale bread you've been munching on for your strength and instead come to *his* banquet.

Two metaphors are given for the feast God wants to refresh us with: wine and milk. Wine is used figuratively in numerous ways in Scripture: It's often illustrated as something that revitalizes and stimulates the soul. It also becomes a symbol of Christ's blood, poured out for us on the cross. And in Israel, milk was more than a drink for kids. It was considered a significant source of nourishment and nutrition for all ages.

We find ourselves thirsting for many other things in life—to have a bigger house with no screaming kids, to have a job that pays more, to be thinner, to be like "her"—only to find we are still unsatisfied. As Isaiah asks, "Why spend your money on food that does not give you strength?" God offers us nourishment and revitalization for our thirsty souls that meets our ultimate need. The wine (Christ's blood) heals, redeems, and restores us. And the milk is God's comfort and love.

scripture discussion questions

In groups of four or five, discuss these questions:

Q: Water is a basic necessity for existence. Why do you think it isn't listed?

Q: God's nonphysical "food" strengthens, nourishes, and brings refreshment. In the past, what are things you've turned to for your "food" which "[did] you no good"?

Q: What things have you spent time thinking about or doing *this week* that have left you with the feeling of little or no satisfaction?

Q: Was there a time in the past when you really did find your nourishment in God? What was that like?

Q: What attitudes and activities are hindering you from having meaningful silent time to listen to God for this kind of fulfillment?

Q: God's invitation to "come and drink" is free, but what do you need to do to make good on it?

heartfelt tip

A common device in Hebrew writing is the repetition of words in a phrase or passage in order to emphasize the importance of what's being said. "Come" is repeated twice in adjacent phrases in this passage. Isaiah was passionate that his hearers wouldn't just listen but would act—they would *come* and *accept* God's free invitation for nourishment and refreshment in an intimate relationship with him.

Take Action

Let's not just *talk* about reflecting on what we need to turn away from in order to experience true intimacy with God, *let's do it!* Write below how you're going to listen to God and receive strength, nourishment, and refreshment. If you're having a hard time thinking of something, choose one of the ideas below. Next week, you'll share with one another how you did.

this week

○ In order to seek my refreshment in God, I'm going to turn away from:

....

....

....

○ I'm going to go with paper and pen to "my place" where I can be quiet and think. I'll identify everything I know that is keeping me from refreshment and intimacy in my relationship with God.

○ I commit to study one of the passages in God's Word this week from the Still Thirsty section (found at the end of this lesson). The first two readings, I'll read to gain a basic understanding of the content. During the third reading, I'll slow way down, really paying attention to its overall message. During the fourth reading, I'll listen to phrases God calls to my attention, mark them, and act in obedience to them.

○ I'll have a week of silence. Instead of listening to music in the car or always having the TV on in the house, I'll spend more time in silence, listening for God's voice.

Prayer

End your time together in prayer to your Father.
Read Psalm 46:10 together.

> *Be still, and know that I am God!*

Be still. Take a deep breath and invite God into what concerns you at this moment: worries, schedules, fears, and pressures. Allow enough time to pray silently for a moment about these. Your hostess will then lead you to say aloud, "Know that I am God." Say it twice to let it sink in. Allow some meaningful silent time to listen to how God wants you to believe in him concerning your situation. Your hostess will close in prayer for the concerns of your heart.

Girlfriend Time

Remember those stories you started sharing with each other in the Experience section? We all love to tell our stories, so get back together with your partner or get in smaller groups and spend time sharing more about your story with each other. Let this time help prepare you for turning away from the noise of life as you take time to really listen to each other.

Still Thirsty?

If you're still thirsty to know more about finding refreshment in God, check out these Scriptures:

Revelation 3:17-20

"You say, 'I am rich. I have everything I want. I don't need a thing!' And you don't realize that you are wretched and miserable and poor and blind and naked. So I advise you to buy gold from me—gold that has been purified by fire. Then you will be rich. Also buy white garments from me so you will not be shamed by your nakedness, and ointment for your eyes so you will be able to see. I correct and discipline everyone I love. So be diligent and turn from your indifference.

"Look! I stand at the door and knock. If you hear my voice and open the door, I will come in, and we will share a meal together as friends."

Q: When you try to be self-sufficient, what are the results? List all the results Jesus promises when we turn to him.

Matthew 13:15

"For the hearts of the people are hardened, and their ears cannot hear, and they have closed their eyes—so their eyes cannot see, and their ears cannot hear, and their hearts cannot understand, and they cannot turn to me and let me heal them."

Q: Rewrite this verse from a positive perspective and personalize it. Reflect on what you've written. What hope do you find?

Matthew 7:24-27

"Anyone who listens to my teaching and follows it is wise, like a person who builds a house on solid rock. Though the rain comes in torrents and the floodwaters rise and the winds beat against that house, it won't collapse because it is built on bedrock. But anyone who hears my teaching and ignores it is foolish, like a person who builds a house on sand. When the rains and floods come and the winds beat against that house, it will collapse with a mighty crash."

Q: When you listen to God, even during the storms of life, how does your perspective change?

John 7:37-38

"On the last day, the climax of the festival, Jesus stood and shouted to the crowds, 'Anyone who is thirsty may come to me! Anyone who believes in me may come and drink! For the Scriptures declare, "Rivers of living water will flow from his heart." ' "

Q: Jesus gives the same invitation to "come and drink" as is given in Isaiah. What is this "living water," and what will it do?

Psalm 107:4-9

"Some wandered in the wilderness, lost and homeless. Hungry and thirsty, they nearly died. 'Lord, help!' they cried in their trouble, and he rescued them from their distress. He led them straight to safety, to a city where they could live. Let them praise the Lord for his great love and for the wonderful things he has done for them. For he satisfies the thirsty and fills the hungry with good things."

Q: What benefits do you find here for accepting God's invitation to "come"?

Renew

Being Renewed by God's Healing

Note to the Hostess:

Baa…Have fun with a sheep theme at this session. Create a pasture of treats for women by sticking various veggies on toothpicks. Then stick these in rows into green Styrofoam (your pasture), and serve them with dips. For example, you could have several rows of baby carrots and several rows of cauliflower clusters (which could certainly pass for tiny sheep), and several rows of cherry tomatoes.

Or you can make a lamb-shaped cake (all kinds of creative ideas can be found on the Internet, in party books, cake decorating books, or recipe books). Whatever you do, make it fun for you and your friends!

This session's passage is all about the peace of God's healing—pleasant pastures and peaceful streams. Imbue your meeting area with this ambience by lighting "fresh air" or "clean breeze" scented candles and playing peaceful music.

Get It...Got It?...Good.

- "fresh air" candles
- lamb-shaped cake or veggies, toothpicks, dips, and stiff green Styrofoam
- peaceful music and CD player for the Experience
- healing hand cream for Girlfriend Time (optional)

Mingling

Start by praying something like this:

> *God, you've been faithful in helping us through this week. Thank you for each woman here. Thank you that you're our good shepherd and we can find loving renewal through your healing in our lives.*

Enjoy the refreshments. Today you'll be considering God's renewal and healing. Speaking of healing, share with each other your best scar story. Show the scar (if appropriate!) and tell the story behind it. Then share with each other how you did this past week in turning away from the things that keep you from refreshment and intimacy with God. (You might want to get in small groups or pairs to discuss this.)

Experience

(Note: The hostess will prepare this experience.) So often we lose perspective of how God views us. Maybe some have never known the truth about who we are in God's eyes. Enjoy this experience that will give you a tiny glimpse of how God wants to rid you of anxiety and discouragement so you'll have renewed spiritual vitality.

Choose a partner and give each other a shoulder massage for two to three minutes while peaceful music is playing. While you gently massage away the tension, tell your partner something encouraging about her. When receiving the massage, keep your eyes closed so you can concentrate on being refreshed.

Ahh…Who could ever turn down a shoulder massage!

Q: How did you feel before the massage? after?

Q: What two words describe how you felt hearing something encouraging about yourself?

Q: Name a time you would have liked to experience healing like this.

the Word

Read Psalm 23 together:

Psalm 23

The Lord is my shepherd; I have all that I need.
He lets me rest in green meadows;
he leads me beside peaceful streams.
He renews my strength.
He guides me along right paths, bringing honor to his name.
Even when I walk through the darkest valley,
I will not be afraid, for you are close beside me.
Your rod and your staff protect and comfort me.

You prepare a feast for me in the presence of my enemies.
You honor me by anointing my head with oil.
My cup overflows with blessings.
Surely your goodness and unfailing love will pursue me all the days of my life,
and I will live in the house of the Lord forever.

a closer look

Read this box anytime to take a deeper look at the verses for this session.

Did you know that sheep are considered to be the highest maintenance of any livestock? They have very specific requirements to survive and can't make it without a shepherd. Rapidly grazing a meadow to barrenness and quickly prone to disease, shepherds have to constantly lead their sheep to new pastures. They won't lie down unless they're free from fear, aren't hungry, are getting along with the other sheep, and have no pests bothering them. They're also prone to wander and are vulnerable to attack from predators. Even if there aren't any wolves lurking, sheep are often "cast down," meaning they're turned over on their backs—and can't get up.

So why are *we* compared to sheep? Hmm…high maintenance, vulnerable, prone to wander, helpless, easily stressed, cast down. Sound familiar? But that's not where the similarities end. Nothing comforts and calms a sheep like the voice, presence, and care of its shepherd. And nothing heals and comforts us like the love, security, and rest we find in God, *our* shepherd.

scripture discussion questions

In groups of four or five, discuss these questions:

Q: God lets us rest in green meadows and leads us by peaceful streams. What are the meadows and streams in your life that God has given you to rest in?

Q: What are the needs that God as shepherd wants to supply for you?

Q: Once we've come to God and he's renewed us, he'll take our hands and lead us on the right path. Is it easy to be a sheep and follow God, or do you find yourself still wandering away occasionally? Explain.

Q: This psalm says God renews our strength—he wants to heal us. Where do you need healing in your life?

Q: What are some things in your life or circumstances that are keeping you from experiencing renewal through God's healing right now?

Q: What steps do you need to take to receive God's healing?

heartfelt tip

Read the first several lines of the psalm again. Notice a progression? 1. God lets me rest. 2. He renews my strength. 3. He guides me along right paths. When we come to God weak and weary, *first* he gives us rest. He knows we need it. *Then* he strengthens and heals us. He builds us back up. And *lastly*, he guides us along his path. He knows we're ready to start walking again, so he takes our hands and takes those first steps with us.

Take Action

Let's not just *talk* about turning to God for healing, *let's do it!* Write below how you're going to trust God enough to allow him to renew and guide you this week. If you're having a hard time thinking of something, choose one of the ideas below. Next week, you'll share with one another how you did.

this week

○ I'm going to allow God to heal me by:

....

....

....

....

○ I'm going to list all my fears about trusting God with the circumstances of my life. I'll then choose to trust that I will be renewed; I'll lie down and rest in peace.

○ I commit to follow God in his right paths and his timing by the choices I make this week (even if that means to wait).

○ I'll put a Band-Aid on the back of my hand (a fresh one each day). When I see this, it will remind me to talk to God and give him one area in my life in which I need healing. I'll completely entrust it to him and know that he will restore me.

Prayer

End your time together in prayer to your Father.
Read Proverbs 3:5-6 together.

> Trust in the Lord with all your heart; do not depend on your own understanding.
> Seek his will in all you do, and he will show you which path to take.

Form small groups of two or three and pray for each other, considering these thoughts: God takes us where he wants us to go and gives us direction to see our path only as far ahead as we need to see. He wants us to trust him. He'll lead us safely and securely to healing. Ask him for faith to follow where he leads, to not run ahead of him or lag behind. Thank him for his secure direction in your life today!

Girlfriend Time

Want a real-life experience of what healing is like? Cleanse your hands with soap and water. Choose partners, and take turns applying a dab of hand cream to the hands of your partner and massaging one another's hands. As you gently rub away the dry skin, talk about a time when someone (God or another person) did something for you that helped you heal. Let this time renew you to face the circumstances and activities of your life this week.

Still Thirsty?

If you're still thirsty to know more about God's healing through renewal, check out these Scriptures:

John 10:9-11, 14-15

"Yes, I am the gate. Those who come in through me will be saved. They will come and go freely and will find good pastures. The thief's purpose is to steal and kill and destroy. My purpose is to give them a rich and satisfying life. I am the good shepherd. The good shepherd sacrifices his life for the sheep…I am the good shepherd; I know my own sheep, and they know me, just as my Father knows me and I know the Father. So I sacrifice my life for the sheep."

Q: Describe your life outside the sheepfold of Jesus. In what ways does he give you a rich and satisfying life by passing through his gate?

John 12:40

"The Lord has blinded their eyes and hardened their hearts—so that their eyes cannot see, and their hearts cannot understand, and they cannot turn to me and have me heal them."

Q: Is there something in your life that is keeping you from seeing and hearing God and receiving his healing?

Isaiah 43:1, 18-21

"But now, O Jacob, listen to the Lord who created you. O Israel, the one who formed you says, 'Do not be afraid, for I have ransomed you. I have called you by name; you are mine.'"

"But forget all that—it is nothing compared to what I am going to do. For

I am about to do something new. See, I have already begun! Do you not see it? I will make a pathway through the wilderness. I will create rivers in the dry wasteland. The wild animals in the fields will thank me, the jackals and owls, too, for giving them water in the desert. Yes, I will make rivers in the dry wasteland so my chosen people can be refreshed. I have made Israel for myself, and they will someday honor me before the whole world."

Q: What did you find here that could calm your fears and bring refreshment to you?

Isaiah 40:31

"But those who trust in the Lord will find new strength. They will soar high on wings like eagles. They will run and not grow weary. They will walk and not faint."

Q: We all feel weak at times and need to be renewed with strength. What condition does God give for you to receive strength? Rewrite this verse in your own words, personalizing it based on your circumstances.

Lamentations 3:22-24

"The faithful love of the Lord never ends! His mercies never cease. Great is his faithfulness; his mercies begin afresh each morning. I say to myself, 'The Lord is my inheritance; therefore, I will hope in him!' "

Q: What refreshment do you find here that offers you hope?

Rejoice

Celebrating God's Love

Note to the Hostess:

Because the women may be coming from chaotic, demanding schedules and difficult pressures, treat them like princesses so they can look above their circumstances and rejoice in God's love! Have a royal tea party. Women will celebrate that God, the King of kings, wants us for his own daughters.

Welcome your group of princesses with a sign on your front door that says, "Welcome to the Royal Tea Party!" Serve scrumptious scones with lemon curd, whipped butter, and jams. To drink, serve flavored teas and lemonade. If you'd like, serve other little pastries, too. You could even make or purchase tiaras for each woman or give each a candy ring. Pick a favorite classical music CD to play in the background. Read the Experience section to find out how to prepare.

Get It...Got It?...Good.

- scones or other pastries with lemon curd, jam, and whipped butter
- flavored teas, lemonade
- royal décor, such as tiaras, candy rings, and a welcome sign
- classical music via radio or CD
- assorted small rocks or stones for the Experience section
- manicure supplies for Girlfriend Time (optional)

Mingling

Before starting, pray something like this:

> *God, thank you for each of your precious daughters here. We need your help to understand that you love us and we are your princesses. You're in control of all our circumstances so we can celebrate! In Jesus' name, amen.*

Revel in royalty together enjoying your tea and finger desserts. As you sip and nibble, tell one another the time you felt most like royalty (maybe at your wedding or on a vacation or when you were a little girl). Then tell one another how you allowed God to heal you this week and how you experienced renewal.

Experience

(Note: The hostess will prepare this experience.) Buy enough small stones or rocks for each woman to have one. Visit rock shops (buy from the inexpensive bins of rocks), garden centers, or hobby stores to find rocks.

Ask each woman to think about one difficult time she's experienced and how God helped her through it. Then allow each woman to pick a rock from your selection to be her memory stone, symbolizing this time. If you're able to get distinct-looking rocks, ask women to choose rocks that somehow remind them of or symbolize that experience. For example, if it was a time of depression, she can choose a blue rock. They can take these stones home, put them in a visible place, keep them in their pockets, or decorate them. Each time they see them, they'll be reminded to celebrate God's goodness and love.

With partners or small groups, have women discuss these questions:

Q: Feel the edges and surfaces of your rock. Tell about the time God helped you through a rough situation.

Q: Why did you pick this particular rock to be a symbol of your experience?

Q: How would frequently remembering what God did for you during this time change your perspective?

the Word

Read Luke 1:46-55 together:

Luke 1:46-55

Mary responded, "Oh, how my soul praises the Lord. How my spirit rejoices in God my Savior! For he took notice of his lowly servant girl, and from now on all generations will call me blessed. For the Mighty One is holy, and he has done great things for me. He shows mercy from generation to generation to all who fear him. His mighty arm has done tremendous things! He has scattered the proud and haughty ones. He has brought down princes from their thrones and exalted the humble. He has filled the hungry with good things and sent the rich away with empty hands. He has helped his servant Israel and remembered to be merciful. For he made this promise to our ancestors, to Abraham and his children forever."

a closer look

Read this box anytime to take a deeper look at the verses for this session.

As we can see from this passage in Luke, Mary had a great reason to rejoice: She was God's chosen servant to be the mother of the Savior! But she might have faced some of these things, too: public humiliation, burning, or death by stoning. Hmm…*That* could've put a damper on her attitude.

In her culture, Mary's pregnancy could have spelled her doom. She had no reasonable explanation to give her fiancé as to why she wasn't an adulterer. A poor servant girl claiming she'd received a message from an angel that she would conceive the Son of God *might* not be taken seriously. How would you be feeling if you were Mary? Do you think you'd rejoice?

She traveled four to five days to her cousin Elizabeth's house, and was probably pretty tired. (A five-day trip is tiring enough in a car!) She could have been tired, embarrassed, and worried when she reached her family's home. But she didn't show any of this. She was clearly *thrilled.* This passage is what she had to say about her situation. How often do we truly rejoice in God's love even when things *are* going well? Mary certainly didn't let her circumstances get in the way of rejoicing in God's love and favor!

scripture discussion questions

In groups of four or five, discuss these questions:

Q: **List all the things Mary praises God for.**

Q: What does Mary understand about God's character? How would her attitude have been different if she had focused on her uncertain future instead of on God?

Q: How is your outlook regarding your circumstances affecting how you view God?

Q: What are some of the things you have to rejoice in? Anything from the passage?

Q: Mary chose to rejoice in God by saying these words publicly. What can you do to rejoice in God in a way that others will be a part of the celebration, too?

Q: Why do you think God chose Mary specifically to accomplish his purpose? How can you become the kind of servant God uses?

heartfelt tip

Mary's song of praise is similar to Hannah's psalm of praise in 1 Samuel 2:1-10. They were both grateful for God's power because they recognized they could do nothing to change their past, present, or future. They both clearly understood God chose the Israelite nation as his treasured possession despite their size, lack of strength, and fickle loyalty to him. And God chooses you as a daughter despite your shortcomings, too!

Take Action

Let's not just *talk* about rejoicing in God's faithful love for us, *let's do it!* Write below how you're going to rejoice in God and live above your circumstances (make lemonade out of lemons!). If you're having a hard time thinking of something, choose one of the ideas below. Next week, you'll share with one another how you did.

this week

○ I'm going to rejoice in God by:

○ I'm going to write down all the "lemons" in my life. Then I'll write how God used or is using those things to make refreshing "lemonade" in my life. Then I'll thank him for it—while drinking a glass of lemonade.

○ I commit to thinking about whether I'm truly God's child, his princess. If I am, I'll acknowledge his power in my life and ask him to help me rejoice in my identity! If I haven't yet chosen to be his princess, I'll talk with a leader or friend to find out how.

○ I'll keep my memory stone, representing a time God helped me through a difficult time, in my pocket. Each time I feel it, I'll say a prayer of thanks and rejoice in his goodness.

Prayer

End your time together in prayer to your Father.
Read Joshua 4:5-7 together.

He told them, "Go into the middle of the Jordan, in front of the Ark of the Lord your God. Each of you must pick up one stone and carry it out on your shoulder—twelve stones in all, one for each of the twelve tribes of Israel. We will use these stones to build a memorial. In the future your children will ask you, 'What do these stones mean?' Then you can tell them, 'They remind us that the Jordan River stopped flowing when the Ark of the Lord's Covenant went across.' These stones will stand as a memorial among the people of Israel forever."

As you pray, hold your memory stones in your hands. Thank him for how much he loves you and helps you. Let others hear what you are grateful for!

Girlfriend Time

Since you're all princesses, hang out after the session for some pampering. Set out manicure tools, such as cotton balls, nail polish, nail polish remover, emery boards, and bowls of water. Enjoy some girl time doing your nails while you enjoy each other's friendship.

Still Thirsty?

If you're still thirsty to know more about rejoicing in God's love, check out these Scriptures:

Philippians 4:4

"Always be full of joy in the Lord. I say it again—rejoice!"

Q: Various Scriptures tell us to rejoice. Why do you think we're commanded to worship this way?

Romans 5:2-3

"Because of our faith, Christ has brought us into this place of undeserved privilege where we now stand, and we confidently and joyfully look forward to sharing God's glory. We can rejoice, too, when we run into problems and trials, for we know that they help us develop endurance."

Q: We're to rejoice not only in God's goodness, but also when experiencing trials. Is there a trial in your life you need to rejoice in? How exactly do you do that?

Nehemiah 8:10b

"Don't be dejected and sad, for the joy of the Lord is your strength."

Q: How does joy make you strong?

Jeremiah 29:11

" 'For I know the plans I have for you,' says the Lord. 'They are plans for good and not for disaster, to give you a future and a hope.' "

Q: This promise was given during extremely difficult times for the Jewish people. What can it mean for you today?

Ephesians 1:3-8

"All praise to God, the Father of our Lord Jesus Christ, who has blessed us with every spiritual blessing in the heavenly realms because we are united with Christ. Even before he made the world, God loved us and chose us in Christ to be holy and without fault in his eyes. God decided in advance to adopt us into his own family by bringing us to himself through Jesus Christ. This is what he wanted to do, and it gave him great pleasure. So we praise God for the glorious grace he has poured out on us who belong to his dear Son. He is so rich in kindness and grace that he purchased our freedom with the blood of his Son and forgave our sins. He has showered his kindness on us, along with all wisdom and understanding."

Q: What are some indications from these verses that we can have the same unwavering assurance of God's love that Mary had?

Relationship

.........Finding Refreshment in Relationships.........

Note to the Hostess:

The Experience section may take some of your guests out of their comfort zones, so the atmosphere needs to be inviting. Use dim lighting accented with candles, and soft, relaxing background music. Your willing participation and enthusiasm for the experience will go a long way in encouraging the others to participate. Read the Experience section before the meeting in order to prepare.

This session, women will learn about having humility in their relationships, so serve up some humble pie! Use simple old recipes, such as chess pie, Indian pudding, plum pudding, shoofly pie, or mock apple pie. Make a little sign labeled, "Humble Pie," and place near your pie (or pies). Serve coffee or water on the side.

Get It...Got It?...Good.

- humble pie and small sign
- soft lighting and music
- plastic tubs (can be purchased at a discount store for around $1.00 each), one for every two women
- washcloth and hand or small bath towel, one per person
- peppermint foot soak or fresh-smelling bubble bath and foot cream
- peppermint foot mask for Girlfriend Time (bought or made, optional)

Mingling

Before eating, begin by praying something like this:

> God, thank you for your faithful love to us this week. Thank you for each special friend here. Help us to learn what true relationship means by bringing refreshment to others. In Jesus' name, amen.

This week, enjoy your snacks in a little different way... Serve each other the goodies provided! While you're eating your humble pie, tell one another about the most humble person you've ever known. Then share what you did last week to remember and rejoice in God's faithful love.

Experience

(Note: The hostess will prepare this experience.) Do you want to serve others? Refresh them? Well, here's your chance. This activity may be different from anything you've ever experienced before—you're going to wash each other's feet. It'll give you a better understanding of just how far Jesus wants you to go in refreshing others.

Form pairs. Choose one woman to be the first foot washer. Fill a plastic tub with warm water, and add a peppermint-scented foot soak or a little bubble bath while your partner removes her shoes and socks. Kneel in front of your partner as she is seated in a chair. Use the washcloth to wash both feet. (If you're feeling especially servant-like you can even give them a little rub.) Dry them individually in a hand or small bath towel. Apply peppermint foot cream.

The woman having her feet washed will share an area in which she needs prayer. As you finish up, pray for God to show his faithful love to her in her situation. Then switch roles and repeat!

With partners or small groups, have women discuss these questions:

Q: Tell in one word or one phrase what it felt like to have your feet washed.

Q: How did it feel to have one person fully focused on you and serving you?

Q: Tell about a time you were able to refresh a friend.

the Word

Read John 13:12-15 together:

John 13:12-15

    After washing their feet, he put on his robe again and sat down and asked, "Do you understand what I was doing? You call me 'Teacher' and 'Lord,' and you are right, because that's what I am. And since I, your Lord and Teacher, have washed your feet, you ought to wash each other's feet. I have given you an example to follow. Do as I have done to you."

a closer look

Read this box anytime to take a deeper look at the verses for this session.

Today's Scripture shows how we should treat our friends—we're to refresh them and be refreshed by them. Jesus taught his disciples a powerful lesson using a very common practice in the culture of his day. But he did it in a very uncommon way—he washed their feet!

Does the idea of washing a friend's feet *today* make you shudder? In Jesus' day, feet weren't nearly so nicely kept. Traveling by foot on dry, dusty roads in open sandals, feet had many chances to get dirty. So, at the entrance of a dwelling, it was the role of the servant to perform the menial task of foot washing before entering the living quarters. A superior *never* washed the feet of an inferior. Humility wasn't a great virtue in those days. The Romans of the day despised the concept of humility and Greeks despised menial labor. Jesus, as a great teacher of the time, would have been expected to sit back and be served by others. Not so! He did the opposite, choosing to forgo his rights, humble himself, and refresh others. (And he continued acts of self-sacrifice until it culminated in the ultimate sacrifice, his death on the cross.)

scripture discussion questions

In groups of four or five, discuss these questions:

Q: How do you think the disciples were feeling as Jesus washed their feet? If Jesus were here today to wash your feet, how would it make you feel?

Q: Often times, when we think of serving others, we think of helping people less fortunate than us. But Jesus washed the feet of his friends. Does it make you more or less comfortable to think of serving *friends* in this way?

Q: What's one way that a friend has refreshed you recently?

Q: God refreshes us, but he also gives us friends to fulfill the role of refresher. What are you missing out on when you're not refreshing friends or accepting their refreshment?

Q: What do you think the balance is between finding your refreshment in Jesus and being refreshed by friends?

Q: Refreshing others, as Jesus refreshed, involves sacrifice. What's one way you can refresh your friends in a way that involves personal sacrifice?

heartfelt tip

Humility can easily be misunderstood as weakness. If you don't demand your rights or make other people serve you, you're weak, right? Wrong. The strongest person is the one who doesn't need to bring attention to herself or defend her rights—it's strength in knowing that God is taking care of you. We're called to quietly, humbly follow Christ's example of service toward others, and when we do, we bring him glory!

Take Action

Let's not just *talk* about bringing refreshment to others, *let's do it!* Write below how you're going to humbly serve others. If you're having a hard time thinking of something, choose one of the ideas below. Next week, you'll share with one another how you did.

this week

○ I'm going to humbly bring refreshment to others by:

....

....

....

....

○ I'm going to look for small ways to deny my own rights and help a friend. I might do a load of laundry for a friend, pull weeds for a friend, or call a friend who I know is down, even though I'd rather read a book.

○ I'll consider and pray about a friendship in which I've felt wronged. In prayer, I'll humbly forgive them. If I need to address the issue with the friend, I'll kindly approach that person and ask to talk things over.

○ If I have a hard time accepting help from others, I'll let my guard down and humbly allow my friends to refresh me when they try.

Prayer

End your time together in prayer to your Father.
Read Philippians 2:3-5 together.

> Don't be selfish; don't try to impress others. Be humble, thinking of others as better than yourselves. Don't look out only for your own interests, but take an interest in others, too. You must have the same attitude that Christ Jesus had.

Take several minutes to think in silence about an area in your life in which you've been prideful recently. Silently ask God for forgiveness. Pray together for strength from God to humbly serve each other this week in ways that will bring refreshment.

Girlfriend Time

Since your tootsies are already in pampering mode and you've got the tubs filled with water, do some foot masks. (Kind of like face masks for the feet!) You can buy foot masks at beauty supply stores or make your own mask. Here's a simple recipe for one mask: Mix 1/2 ripe avocado, 1 tablespoon sesame oil, 1 tablespoon plain yogurt in a blender. Apply to feet and leave on for 10 minutes; then rinse off in warm water. (You could even bring the supplies and have women make their own mask.) While you sit back and relax, talk about how *you* would most like to be refreshed, and then think of ways you can bring that kind of refreshment to others.

Still Thirsty?

If you're still thirsty to know more about how relationship blossoms in humble service to others, check out these Scriptures:

John 15:12-17

"This is my commandment: Love each other in the same way I have loved you. There is no greater love than to lay down one's life for one's friends. You are my friends if you do what I command. I no longer call you slaves, because a master doesn't confide in his slaves. Now you are my friends, since I have told you everything the Father told me. You didn't choose me. I chose you. I appointed you to go and produce lasting fruit, so that the Father will give you whatever you ask for, using my name. This is my command: Love each other."

Q: We are Jesus' friends if we do what he says: Love one another and lay down your life for your friends. How far are you willing to go to love your friends?

Philippians 2:5-8

"You must have the same attitude that Christ Jesus had. Though he was God, he did not think of equality with God as something to cling to. Instead, he gave up his divine privileges; he took the humble position of a slave and was born as a human being. When he appeared in human form, he humbled himself in obedience to God and died a criminal's death on a cross."

Q: Christ is our example of how we're to treat others—he denied his rights and became a humble slave. What do your relationships look like when you deny yourself and others become the primary focus? Which attitude brings greater satisfaction: self-focus or self-denial?

Matthew 25:37-40

"Then these righteous ones will reply, 'Lord, when did we ever see you hungry and feed you? Or thirsty and give you something to drink? Or a stranger and show you hospitality? Or naked and give you clothing? When did we ever see you sick or in prison and visit you?' And the King will say, 'I tell you the truth, when you did it to one of the least of these my brothers and sisters, you were doing it to me!' "

Q: How can you begin to see others through Jesus' eyes of compassion? What change would you need to make to show this kind of compassion to others?

Luke 22:24-27

"Then they began to argue among themselves about who would be the greatest among them. Jesus told them, 'In this world the kings and great men lord it over their people, yet they are called "friends of the people." But among you it will be different. Those who are the greatest among you should take the lowest rank, and the leader should be like a servant. Who is more important, the one who sits at the table or the one who serves? The one who sits at the table, of course. But not here! For I am among you as one who serves.' "

Q: What do you sometimes do to be seen as important by others? Name one habit or attitude that you could change to serve others better.

Romans 12:9-10

"Don't just pretend to love others. Really love them. Hate what is wrong. Hold tightly to what is good. Love each other with genuine affection, and take delight in honoring each other."

Q: Think of someone you have had difficulty getting along with. What are specific actions you could take to improve your relationship? How can you honor that person?

Refreshment

Becoming Messengers of Refreshment

Note to the Hostess:

This is your last session together, so make the atmosphere energetic and fun—think water and balloons. (No, not necessarily together!) Use fun background music or music with water sounds. Set out desk fountains. See if your church nursery or someone you know has a bubble machine you could borrow. For added festivity, have bunches of bright balloons around your meeting area. Give one to each friend when she leaves.

For a refreshing snack, have your favorite fruit smoothie recipe prepared, in glasses filled about ⅔ full, complete with a fruit garnish on the glass and fun straws. Women can add their own "sparkle" with lemon-lime soda or ginger ale. Read the Experience section to find out how to prepare before the session.

Get It...Got It?...Good.

- water machines, desk fountain, or music with water sounds, and balloons for festive décor
- fruit smoothies, fresh fruit garnish, straws, and lemon-lime soda or ginger ale
- for every 4 people: I tall clear 12-ounce glass or plastic cup, I cup white vinegar, I teaspoon baking soda, several grapes, I plastic spoon for Experience
- pens for Girlfriend Time (optional)

Mingling

Before you refresh your taste buds with your sparkling fruit smoothies, pray something like this:

Thank you, God, for giving us the opportunity to spend this time together with friends. Thank you for what we've learned about how to experience your healing and love. Help us to be your messengers, sharing your refreshment with others. In Jesus' name, amen.

As you sip your smoothies, begin sharing with each other using this sentence:

This week God helped me to refresh someone by...

Experience

(Note: The hostess will prepare this experience.) Think of a time you received wonderful news from someone you knew you could trust. How did it make you feel? This activity will help you see firsthand how when we are refreshed in Christ, we can lift each other up in refreshment, too.

Get in groups of four or five. Over a protected area, fill a clear, tall 12-ounce glass with 1 cup of vinegar. Add several grapes. Carefully add ½ teaspoon of baking soda, stirring a little if necessary. If nothing happens to the grapes, add ¼ teaspoon more. Spend a few minutes carefully observing. Then, add one additional ¼ teaspoon baking soda.

With partners or small groups, have women discuss these questions:

Q: What happened to the grapes before you added the baking soda?

Q: What happened after adding baking soda? Did adding additional baking soda have an effect on the grapes?

Q: In a spiritual sense, if the grapes represent us, what would the baking soda represent? What would the bubbles represent? How is this like or unlike how Christ refreshes you?

Q: When have you received this kind of refreshment? When have you given it to others?

the Word

Read Proverbs 25:13 and John 7:37-39 together:

Proverbs 25:13

Trustworthy messengers refresh like snow in summer. They revive the spirit of their employer.

John 7:37-39

On the last day, the climax of the festival, Jesus stood and shouted to the crowds, "Anyone who is thirsty may come to me! Anyone who believes in me may come and drink! For the Scriptures declare, 'Rivers of living water will flow from his heart.' " (When he said "living water," he was speaking of the Spirit, who would be given to everyone believing in him. But the Spirit had not yet been given, because Jesus had not yet entered into his glory.)

a closer look

Read this box anytime to take a deeper look at the verses for this session.

These Scriptures are an invitation from Christ to be refreshed and in turn refresh others with his living water. Let's discover why his offer was so significant.

The Feast of Tabernacles celebrated how God brought water out of the rock to satisfy the complaining Israelites (Numbers 20:8-11). During this feast, the priests performed a solemn ritual, symbolic of this ancient event. Every day for seven days, there was a procession from the Temple to the Pool of Siloam. A priest would fill his gold pitcher from the pool while a choir sang Isaiah 12:3, "With joy you will drink deeply from the fountain of salvation." The priests would then march around the Temple altar. On the seventh day, the *greatest* day, they marched around the altar seven times chanting Psalm 118:25, "Please, Lord, please save us. Please, Lord, please give us success."

It was probably during the climax of this ritual when Christ stood in a dramatic moment and shouted his invitation to drink from his living water. He revealed at that moment that he was the fulfillment of the prophecy, "you will drink deeply from the fountain of salvation." And he was the answer to the prayer, "Lord, please save us." The water from the rock in Numbers and the Feast of Tabernacles were a part of God's plan to lead up to and foreshadow the salvation he would offer in Jesus. Jesus says, "Come to me"; he is God's plan for *all* to come and be renewed in him.

scripture discussion questions

In groups of four or five, discuss these questions:

Q: What is the living water Jesus is referring to? What exactly is Jesus offering here?

Q: Describe spiritual thirst. When was a time you were really thirsty for God's refreshment?

Q: Think about your life right now. Imagine experiencing the solemn, all-too-familiar ritual described in this passage year after year, and then hearing Jesus shout his invitation to all who could hear. How do you think you would respond to this unexpected "interruption"?

Q: "Trustworthy messengers refresh like snow in summer." If you're God's messenger, do you think faithfully delivering his message refreshes and revives others? If so, how?

Q: The living water Jesus referred to is the Holy Spirit. What role does the Holy Spirit play and what role do we play in delivering Christ's message?

Q: What do you think being God's messenger, delivering the message "come and drink," looks like? How can you become a more trustworthy messenger?

heartfelt tip

Virgin's Spring was the only source of fresh water for the city of Jerusalem. In order to get the water to the Pool of Siloam and keep the water from enemies during a siege, a huge feat needed to be accomplished: A conduit was dug through solid rock that was 1,780 feet long!

What a feat—a channel the length of five football fields cut through solid rock to bring refreshing water to the people. It's a beautiful visual representation of "rivers of living water [flowing] from his heart." How much more wondrous was the feat of God's sacrifice to bring us this water and the power of the Holy Spirit to refresh us!

Take Action

It's not just talk about being messengers of Christ's refreshment, *let's do it!* Write below how you're going to refresh others with Christ's living water. If you're having a hard time thinking of something, choose one of the ideas below.

this week

I'm going to be a messenger of Christ's refreshment by:

....

....

....

....

I'm going to make sure I've accepted Jesus' message to come and drink by spending some time praying with God and talking honestly with him about where my heart is.

I'm going to share how Christ's living water has changed my life with one other person—over glasses of iced tea or another cold and refreshing beverage.

I'll keep a container of minty-fresh breath mints handy this week. Every time I pop one into my mouth and experience a burst of refreshment, I'll thank God for a different friend and ask God to bring refreshment to her this week. Perhaps God will even use me to be that source of refreshment!

Prayer

End your time together in prayer to your Father. Read this as a prayer for each other as you end your study together: Numbers 6:24-26.

> *May the Lord bless you and protect you. May the Lord smile on you and be gracious to you. May the Lord show you his favor and give you his peace.*

In the past six weeks, we've learned to rest in Jesus, find healing, rejoice in his love, be humble friends, and now how to share his refreshment with others! Let's thank him for his loving care in our lives.

Girlfriend Time

In these six weeks, you and your girlfriends have grown in relationships with each other and, more importantly, with God. You'll want a memory of that, so use the Refreshing Memories pages at the end of this book to commemorate your time together. If you're in a larger group, you may want to get in groups of four or five to do this activity.

Write your name at the bottom of your page; then pass it to your right. As you receive others' books, think of one important lesson you learned or insight you gained during your six weeks together and write this on the page, along with your name and phone number or e-mail address. Pass it to the right. Continue to write and pass the books until each of you has a page full of meaningful thoughts. Use this for encouragement, to pray for one another, and to keep building those friendships. While writing, chat about how the past six weeks have affected you.

heartfelt tip

You've all grown closer to Jesus and each other by now, and that's pretty special! If you'd like a memento of your time together, get this Heart-Spa pewter charm for yourself and your girlfriends. The verse will remind you that we can *always* turn to Jesus for our rest.

Still Thirsty?

If you're still thirsty to know more about how Christ's living water brings refreshment to you and through you to others, check out these Scriptures:

1 Thessalonians 1:5

"For when we brought you the Good News, it was not only with words but also with power, for the Holy Spirit gave you full assurance that what we said was true."

Q: How can you make sure that your efforts to share Jesus' message with others is done through the power of the Holy Spirit?

Isaiah 58:11

"The Lord will guide you continually, giving you water when you are dry and restoring your strength. You will be like a well-watered garden, like an ever-flowing spring."

Q: Imagine a trustworthy messenger delivering this message to you. How would this message most help you right now?

Psalm 42:1-2

"As the deer longs for streams of water, so I long for you, O God. I thirst for God, the living God. When can I go and stand before him?"

Q: What creates the sensation of spiritual thirst in you? Does knowing that others may have this same thirst motivate you to be a faithful messenger?

Psalm 1:1-3

"Oh, the joys of those who do not follow the advice of the wicked, or stand around with sinners, or join in with mockers. But they delight in the law of the Lord, meditating on it day and night. They are like trees planted along the riverbank, bearing fruit each season. Their leaves never wither, and they prosper in all they do."

Q: We are compared to trees along a riverbank. What makes these trees healthy? Think of a spiritual "tree" you have known. How did this person refresh you? What refreshment can you offer to others?

Galatians 5:22-23

"But the Holy Spirit produces this kind of fruit in our lives: love, joy, peace, patience, kindness, goodness, faithfulness, gentleness, and self-control. There is no law against these things!"

Q: Think of a relationship or situation in your life that isn't going so well. Describe how your actions and attitudes would be different by applying these evidences of the Holy Spirit in your life.

{RefreshingMemories}

Name: ....

{RefreshingMemories}

Name: ....

{RefreshingMemories}

Name: ....

{RefreshingMemories}

Name: ....